Harmonie

First Edition

Joseph Leo Hickey

Rev. D

Melodium
House

www.MelodiumHouse.com
joseph@melodiumhouse.com

Introductory Information

This book contains a story about a fictional interracial couple from fictional iterations of The United States and South Africa.

Harmonie, a South African political activist was murdered on December 24th, 2019. The murder was motivated by race and political opposition.

A few months later, her husband, Liefie was found dead in the United States, in Chicago. The investigation is pending but is presumed by many that the murder was motivated entirely by race.

Both died for no reason.

Racism is absurd.

These poems are their words.

Key:

Harmonie, Liefie, **Both**

"We [the EFF] are not calling for the slaughter of white people, at least for now."
-Julius Malema

"With a kiss I die."
-Romeo & Juliet

"I have overcome the world."
-Jesus Christ

CD #3

last night i had a dream
we were escaping from the wrath
of the forest fires,
hastening towards us

this morning,
there was so much fear
the moment we heard the gunshots
and we left our hotel room
in the adrenaline rush
now
as we sit hand in hand in the front seats of the car
we kiss our past goodbye forever

we drive through the streets of Durban for the last time
we live in a world so broken
that the people who were assigned to fix it
have left and taken their payment with them

as i waited
for the world to be judged,

i sat in the boxcar

i closed my eyes
and i believed
that the memories i envisioned
were still alive

when i first saw you,
you were standing alone
we spoke
for fifteen minutes
and you told me about life in Durban,
i told you about my plans for the future,

how i would create art
that the whole world would see
and fall in love with

but these memories are interrupted by the lull
movement of the incoming train,
and now
i have more dreams
and nightmares
that you are alive
but you are taken against your will,
somewhere you never wanted to go

but then the memory flashes in again,
we were walking through the streets of the city,
she was spinning in my arms, dancing
in the forest at night,
smiling, laughing
like the galaxies far from here
where there is no death

that these moments existed at all
gives me peace even when they are gone
and Harmonie has passed away

we had packed our bags together
and left the airport
and traveled to Norway the summer when we were married

a spell of darkness that falls over
people when they are dreaming
when they are grieving
when the world moves on,
and we stay stuck in the same motions
unable to move forward
or backward

we sat at a Starbucks together,
drinking coffee,

we made plans that transform
our world
i painted a portrait of Harmonie
and it encapsulated her spirit
i hold it in my hands now
and grasp onto it
as i walk through the south side of Chicago,
my home
where i feel the chemicals
in my mind overflowing,
wishing there was anything else i could do

10,9

all the perfect, holy and beautiful things
joy unfiltered and light uncreated,
grace pouring down on me and lighting my path

we walked by the light of the torches
on the beach at midnight

our hearts sealed forever,

our movements are inseparable from each other
we are dancing across the world,
traversing through the night,
separated and then walking blindly in the night
until we replace the constitution
of our hearts with a book of our own
we will be the signification
of the dawn of a new and glorious era
 when the whole world falls under the banner of the cross
becoming one family
and we will see the beauty in the art of simply falling in love
of desperate and lamenting songs
about everything including joy

sometimes when we walk the path of life
we become lost
we stray from the straight path
i can imagine many people feel the same way
we come home from the night in the city
we are so very vulnerable
there is no part of me that has not touched your soul
we crave connection
with the natural things in this life
more than anything else
with the pattering rain outside
with the ghosts that follow our footsteps
everywhere we go
we become believers in the things we never
thought could exist
at the altar we drink from the cup of our salvation
we forget what races we are
when we become totally united to each other
the leaves cover the path
the shadow follows the light
we have been dreaming all through the night
of crossing bridges we never built
of lifting the world out of the mud with us
leaving no one behind at all
i stand at the terminal of the airport
and then my surroundings change
and then we slowly grow used to the change
until we have cast out all transitional objects
from our lives
when perfect fear casts out love
when there is no music but only books and routine
we are the disempowered,
we are the disenfranchised
we are the ones whose voices will blend
with every innocuous voice in the world
and then i will stand in a country that never listened to me
i will say no more words to this country

because all my breath will be taken from me
and then we will walk through the shadow of these woods
as the sun sets deeper into its place than it ever has
each of us has taken a different road
and each of us has become lost and never reaches our destination
and then the voice of my Liefie will
be filled with so much anger that it will overthrow the world
when he reads the words that i wrote
at every political convention

we will walk through the tall grass
hands outstretched
faces drowning in the sunlight and
bathing in it
i am here if you want me to be here
though i never wanted to be here

the doctors were barely able to remove the bullet
from my shoulder after i had fled for cover

i started writing a letter
and then i started singing the words
and each word poured from my pen
with such poignancy and clarity
the day after we were married
we stood hand in hand on the beach
the candles were all around us
the light from the candles mixed with the stars
was enough to make us desire
to break through from something
beyond the way we look superficially
beyond the way others see us,
to tell them
we are something unique

III

when you come looking for me
you'll find me where you are
i'll be in hell…

you've unleashed a demon onto the world

gunshots,
all of us getting shot
i'm on the other side of the parking lot,
bleeding out from the wounds
the whole world will
burn, you'll all be coming with me
i'm not heinous or cruel
just the truth
rap songs blaring from my speakers
death comes to us and the world is judged
all of you
on the outside looking in

i can hear the angels cry
i can hear heaven fall away
as we realize
what we've lost
and then waste it all away
we understand what will happen now
we are filled with anger now

falling

deeper

    deeper

deeper

spinning the revolver all around
about to take a shot but now,
you'll be listening to the sound so loud
i'll be sitting on the bar stool
and then you hear it coming like a power tool

with such violence
we overthrow the world

112

when you are walking in circles
wondering about what you should do
what you should tell your family
when you learned that your wife is dead

you go to sleep
you sleep on a bed of nails
the first thing
you feel in the cycle of grief

how did
this happen?
because love was transformed into torture

and every single day that goes on from now on
will be lived in a different world than the one
you experienced before
and you will go into this world
greeting it with violent words
because you know when you lost me forever
the world would no longer be the world
the world is drenched in what makes it forget
everything it was made for

when the violence and the anger go away
all that's left is one simple thing
resentment and death
there is something so mournful
you will only find it when you listen closely
when you stop and forget about what you've lost
we create true art when we ourselves are broken

i was pacing across the floor of my apartment
and i did not believe i could go through another year
i felt like i was suffocating
in the worst way
when love is all we have
when the borders of our countries
are broken
and hatred flows out from these borders
when every day that goes by is nothing but
the anxiety that we dread
into forgetting the other more
when our foreign city burns away
we will walk towards that city hand in hand
long after we have passed away

through the alleyways of a broken city
you haven't seen anything yet but a war about to be
unleashed
this desperate shell
where there are no voices,
just darkness pouring over the slums
and rage against the thief masquerading in the night
where we say goodbye to everything that we loved about the
natural world

there are moments
when you think the world will slow down
but the world never does
until our body is ashes
and it is blown apart by the wind
like the unresisting air
because even our names will be forgotten in time
our lifetimes are full of danger
and wrath
but none of it compares to what is inside my soul

you left me for dead,
you threw away the shovel
but i clawed through the dirt
and came back to find you
and you knew when you saw me
that the time had certainly come
for all fate to be fulfilled

once i was drowning in my own tears

from the memories of being alone
at night
after i learned my wife had died

now i've come to challenge you
you and i hear a shotgun blast
and then we know the pain won't last

screams throughout the city
nothing can stop us from surviving

my words will be like violence
but behind my bars,
we are isolated
there is truth you never understood,
there is violent music

as poetic as it is profane,
as deadly as it desires to live

Harmonie walks all the places you were too afraid to walk

as much truth in English
as there was in Afrikaans
as much truth in Afrikaans
as there was in Zulu

there is as much violence in my words in English
as any other language i might have spoken

when words and poetry flow through me like bombs
when i never stop
speaking
the love inside her soul has turned to anger now
you will hear the silent feet of children in Pretoria and
Chicago. these feet walking down the cobbled streets
will echo my name

115

at the end of the world
everyone you kicked
and pushed down with your feet
ascended up
to challenge you
and these people were given a crown
and a kingdom

and you fell down to the bottom
and broke both your legs
and no one was there to help you ever again
and then hell opened wide
and you remembered all the times
you avoided eye contact with us

i have no political affiliation

i am not left or right
i have become something more
than black or white
i felt the blood pulse out of my shoulder
when i learned that Harmonie had been shot
i felt all political affiliation leave me
when i learned that we were all human
i say hello to the criminals
on the street corner
and then i walk past them and don't
say another word
and words flow from me like the movements
of a dance whenever i pick up my pen
whenever i record my voice
i will tell her story

we are going eighty miles per hour down the freeway
and we know we will never stop
yesterday i was in her arms
today i am in the slums of Chicago
we are still at war with the world
we hear the sad violin music in the faces of strangers
we hear the police cars roaring
we hear depth in every syllable
we hear death in every moment
when we think about the future

here's another eulogy for the world that would never listen
here's another eulogy for the world that took a drink of its
own poverty and then died
it drowned in its own lack of inhibition
it lamented its own routine
it marched on until the end
and then we read about it years later
how can you even live with yourself in a world this broken?
how can you not shout words of liberty from the roof of
every building you step on?
how can your pen ever stop moving?

and why did they not listen to a single word you were saying?
i sit in front of the McDonald's
with the last bit of cash i just spent
the last bit of cash left in my bank account

and i know i will never hold a job again
after how devastated i was
we hear the crowds roaring
we hear them begging for the next action to happen
their entertainment will be the death of the world
and they have seen this film a hundred times

as the sirens roar through the street we run away
and then i find myself home, underneath the bridge
where i light a fire in the trash bin
and then wait for the last of my time to expire
because i know at this rate i will not survive any of this
and somewhere in the distance i hear a voice crying out
"unredeemable"
and it was speaking to the world

and then i paced through the city
as if it was my bedroom floor

116

as i drift off
to sleep,
i lay down at peace
because an angel watches over me

as we grow older
we forget our dreams
but the stars
from those dreams
light my path,
i think your stars cross
my stars,
i think your angels are so close to my angels

and that my oceans meet your oceans
in the network of the spirits
we are in union

III

i sit in my room,
feeling the familiar and
unwelcome dullness fall over the world
when i used to be excited
now there is indifference
where there used to be a deep ocean
there is now a shallow pool
we no longer dive into the water
because our feet always hit the bottom
i drift with my mind
and approach places
i never will see in this life
there are desperate souls in this life
there are questions that will never be answered
or even acknowledged,
how years later i know
i will write about this simple
experience
and contemplate it,
during the time i am no longer
bored out of my mind
when i have a job and a wife
and several beautiful children
and we pass our experiences
down one hundred generations

you are
my joy defined
you are the one
i will hold so close to me
and the fears we had
so long ago, they all will
melt away, and float forever

somewhere we can never reach them

building our new life together
we know the world will from now on
forget about its own dysfunction
how none of this ever works
the pieces we tried to put together
would never fit together,
how we were always in the wrong place
at the wrong time
how all luck had run out
and as the rain pours outside
i come in to greet you, with a thousand kisses
and fall asleep with you
into pure amnesia,
forgetting the anxiety of the past

118

i want to get myself so far away
from here,
i want to put myself out to sea
anywhere as far as i can go is fine

if you're screaming out my name
i won't hear you in the dark
no! you won't ever hold me again
i have fallen into poverty

we've fallen so very far
we've eaten up your lies like gasoline
you light the match and soon after
we are dead
you light the match and
you burn our insides out

every screen we look at shows us
a country that longs to be
overthrown
anywhere away from here we go is fine
i'm screaming out for revolution
you can't see me in the black
no! you won't ever notice me again
you are blinded by your heresy

119

we've been told this too many times
we're not going anywhere
here in the dark we waste our lives
but we won't care
there is no more music
there is no expression
here in the dark
we waste our lives
we won't leave our cell

part of me isn't sure what to think
the other part of me is broken
can you reconcile the truth in my stars,
while they are falling from my skies?

we've been separated locked in a cell
we aren't going anywhere
here in the dark our sickness grows
but we won't care
there is no more music
there is no expression
here in the dark we waste our lives
we won't leave our cell

120

we're finding our way home
we're drowning in our past memories
that we couldn't forget if we tried
we're stuck in the valley of the shadow
of regret
and i am in a permanent state of mind

i know you feel it

i know you'll be there when my eyes close
before our last night on earth ends

121

Harmonie wakes me up to see how beautiful
the stars are in the middle of the night

122

there is a shadow
across the bedroom floor
where once was blinding sunlight

24

silence and nothing more
there is a storm inside my heart

123

don't you see me standing here?
don't you hear me scream?

i know you'll be there in the end!
i know my heart is broken!

i feel like i'm dying!
i believe i'm drowning
i know you'll be there in the end!
i know my heart is broken!

124

we came a long way
to get here tonight
while the universe stands still
frozen in ice
Harmonie wears the stars on her skin
i've been waiting forever for this to begin
i'll take you far away from here

*i can feel your heartbeat, let me stay at your side,
falling out of place, hold your heart,
your soul*

*let go of the world you've known
life is waiting on the other side
here by your side
i will never leave
and you'll have a love you've never known*

*we are free
we've been redeemed
everyone stands still*

everyone is stuck
i feel your love on every part of my soul
i've been waiting forever

125

tomorrow morning, i'll hang my head
before i walk beside the shadows
tired of these tantalizing motions
that show me everything beautiful in
a single moment

126

i dream about falling so deep
and i never reach the bottom
of the oceans
and as i sink i admire
the beauty of
the descent into the blue
and then into sheer darkness
where there is nothing left but pure motionlessness
because there will be no more expression

127

walking through the empty city
streets singing, humming about her "ocean eyes"

life grips us and takes us away
and we fall through the many colored sky

where you know the person that will come to save you
will never be me
where you know the person that kisses our children
goodnight
will never be me,

where you know the dreams we share cast their shadow

on an even darker world,
and this world lightens up from the shadows that we cast
because in comparison we are brighter than the sun shining
and we know our truth is offensive to the world
and we know i had a dream; we were sitting on the edge of
the waterfront,
we were drinking
and making fun of all the people who thought they could
bring us down

a thousand times,
over again

the world will rise
and greet the fires,
and be consumed,
be altered
and then be totally transformed
and then the world will be inebriated by the breath of
its own evaporation
and then the world will stand
and then run desperately
away and fall into the arms of those who loved it
but no longer loved it
because the world had an identity crisis
      and didn't realize why it was here
        and didn't realize
          what it needed to do
            a way out of its own
callous shell

and i have scars that have not healed
but the light hides them

i fell in love with her deep blue eyes
they stood alone in mystery,
and her heart was pure and lovely
but because the world didn't understand it
it left her all alone

and as she waited for the world to reject her,
Harmonie wrote a powerful
love letter to the world, saying
no matter how drunk it became
or how many times it wanted to see other people
that she would always be a loyal lover,

but the world was violent to her,
and she ran into my arms
where we promised each other the same things
but kept the promise and never broke it
until the world came back to destroy her

and this sadness grew and the world moved
on from the anger
it had against Harmonie

        because the harmony was gone from the world
for several hundred years
and the world descended into a fit of racism,
inequality and crippling poverty

and we stood afar off and wept
for the world
for what was about to happen to it

128

we became bored of the screens and the television
and instead wanted
to create a world
we could live in and thrive in

we became bored of the tears
that came consistently through the years
because we were beyond broken,
our dead end lives
were nearing the end of the line,

my birds in the desperate dark sea of the world
wanted to leave and could not fly high enough
but eventually your stars
came a little closer and reached down
and let my birds land
where they lived forever
in a land of vibrancy and truth and aspiration

129

when we lay down at night
we are on the total opposite ends of the world
we never looked up at the same moon,
when i see the sun you see the stars
when i see the birds fly, you see the cars
when i feel the freedom, you see the bars

when i reach out for your hand
it never reaches across the world

when i reach out for truth
you hear nothing but poetic lies
when i dream about you
after you're gone,
we no longer see any distinction
between any of us because of our skin color

i have hope,
you fall after me

130

this indifference
this one single moment
where hate is louder
than love

prejudice

that will not
be annihilated
with the firmest
anger,

131

we're broken
and we are leaving
goodbye until
the end of days

132

there is a violinist on the street corner
playing tunes of love
that will be forgotten

the staccato and then
the crescendo
that grows
and diminishes

demonstrating
that our emotions are bursting
out of us
and then they will be silent
and never heard again

133

the rhythm
of the music
which we feel
in our hearts
but never hear
outside of us

Bliss

she wanted a hand to hold
guiding her away from <u>slavery</u>

when she resists
they point the gun at her forehead
she forgets her strength to fight

the bringer of light now gone so far away

when we stare at the walls
of the prison

her skin so fragile

it bursts when it is pricked

when the only
world she knows is one of suffering
beyond comprehension
when her crystal soul is shattered,
when the spreading fires
are extinguished
when we need education,
and to understand
the fallen state of ourselves
the light is defined by the darkness
the flares that light us a path
far from here
spark for a moment
and are extinguished
are buried
and then the world is blind

Father,
no one can hear her,
she is lamenting
the life taken away from a family that loved her
her father
bled out on the hospital
floor

her brother died trying to stop
them from taking her

Son,
she is embalmed in a world
of wild
unendurable
physical pain,
she won't cry anymore

Holy Spirit

the breath of life is fading from her nostrils
while you and i do nothing because we flow
through the world like water with no agency
over our own actions
with no hope for those who are blind

in another world she wears a crown

in another world
Bliss has violently flown away

i want
you to understand
what she
was feeling

she was suffocating,
in the depths
of a vast
and terrifying ocean,
where she
would never be able to fight again
her life was over,

and she finally sank to the bottom
and lived there for the rest of her
life,
where she could not feel the warmth of the sunlight
approaching at all,
where all she could
feel was the cold indifference to despair

where the world had forgotten about her,

she had no strength
she had no emotion
she only felt pain and became so numb to it
that she would not feel anything at all ever again

137

in the depth of a routine
that i found myself in every day

in the moments
where we stand before the unapproachable light
we spill all of our truth
all over the bathroom floor

of our souls
like beer
we spill all our pain
all over the hospital parking lot like
blood
and no one will understand this desperation
no one will understand our need
for connection to others
because we do not know
how to even approach another person
with the truth that we understand
but cannot express

when you cannot promise
to hold on and never let go
because you know you will let go

i was watching Harmonie's speech on the television
about fighting against sex trafficking
the day that she was killed

i was feeling this exasperating
sorrow

i was drowning in my desperation
and then was submerged
and the water of this desperation filled my lungs
until i knew they would never breathe again

i was feeling extreme loneliness
when i knew that the truth in my soul
would go away
when you say you will always
stand by my side
but you have left me and you never come back to me

there is no world
on this or that side of eternity
where the just are the

ones who are wearing crowns

there is no melody i listen to that does not
tell me
to scream out the words

there is no picture too ugly for me to paint a portrait of

there is no world where redemption is unheard of
and not dreamt about day and night

there is no world where redemption is actualized
and is actually attained

there is no orchestra that is unwilling to
champion the melodies Harmonie would gladly
hum back to the rest of the world in her speeches

there is no truth you will not find
in any single one of these things
by simply asking for the truth
and receiving it

there is no drink strong enough
to wash away the pain
because the pain is underneath my soul
and alcohol does not seep through
because nothing can penetrate the upper layer of my soul

there is no drug with the power
to make me desire anything else
than to reconcile us to the world

if you look hard enough you can hear
the voice of God in the spirits of the trees

if you listen closely enough you can see
the desperate souls in the woods
searching for a home they may never find

by using their own strength

they say i've fallen so far away

but today we all realize that none of us understand
anything about anything
except what is underneath our skin
and underneath our very souls

and i have memories
of being alone
in the world
walking through
the forest of it,
finding myself underneath the bridge
and the bottom of the tent is leaking
and we are voicing our dissension
to the deer that are passing by
because we have fallen so far away from
any connection with people

and i sleep in the tent as it fills with water
and dream about
the places i went in my life
before i met Harmonie
and dream about the risks i took in my youth

and the orchestra plays music
the soundtrack of our lives

i cannot find you in the depth of this world
i run after you, but you are never reachable
i dream of finding the truth in your eyes
i dream of overcoming the pain i felt in my youth

i follow you across the train tracks,
but you are so ambivalent

my heart cannot go on much longer
i have descended into the last and worst state of grief

i have become blinded by my dysfunction
will never see a doctor again
will never live a simple life, will always grow closer
to the moments where i know

i held back my punches
i never unleashed my wrath upon the darkness

i know you feel joy when you realize
that the darkness
that you hold so close to you,
will burst with life when it touches your dreary heart
because it will realize what it had done to your heart
and then stop being dark and will embrace
the lovely things of this world

138

we became so drawn to each other
even when we were on opposite sides of the world

we became so united
we became so perfectly beautiful together
that love brought us a peace
the world would not imbibe
and would soon forget
when the voices around were so loud that
they would never listen
i will never stop remembering
the way i feel right now,
the way you make me feel

we need to forget about all the superficial things
that divide us

we need to drive a stake into the heart
of our own
despair
in the moment when we have so much hope
but often ignore it
because we do not understand
what we truly have

we need to be drawn together
in love for all things beautiful

we need to be drawn together
in our infatuation
with the years that are growing
cold, because the coldness
stings our hearts
and makes them fall in love with the warmth
that is remaining in our hearts
until our hearts freeze up and stop
and are not awakened for another
hundred years
and are dazzled
by the rays of light
when the winter finally ends
and the summer breaks through the trees

139

my flag,
my nation

              life

liberty

             and the pursuit of death

her deep blue eyes

             her truth

the consequence
of falling

the consequence
of breathing
so deeply
that your ribs begin
to ache like teeth

the aftermath of a life
lived in such
insatiable

truth

for the very first time
we feel love
as we fall into its ocean
we are very unprepared for love
but let it ravish us
the same

we were very unprepared
for the lives we knew we
had to live separated
and
i was seventeen
when i met you
i was diving into the depths
my iron heart came unglued

i felt like i was swimming
in a deep unfathomable ocean
where for the first of countless times
we would suffocate
and then come alive

and then we would wander the streets
of several cities

        where we knew we would eventually
watch them burn to the ground
after the riots crawling up and down
the once familiar and once lonesome streets

140

as life turned
like a carousel
we found ourselves
in love with the motion of it
as the world moved around us

we stood still,
and we gazed at the passing lights
as in a dream i held the hand of
our son,
and led him to the carousel
of life
where i knew he would
reach out his arms for truth,
for love,
in celebration,
in sorrow
and the understanding of sorrow
in moving and never stopping

141

sometimes i feel
not enough people
can see my paintings
sometimes i feel
bursting with so much
passion, enough to move the world

but then you are with me
in the quiet room,
and i show you everything i have painted
and i am gratified
am falling into truth
and the deepest fulfillment

you would rather read passionate words
to me and me alone
than to have 27 million read your
dull words, and fall in love
with words written without passion
it is better to be hated for being you
than to be loved for being fake
and you wrote words that only
i would read

and they reached into my heart
and never left for the rest of my life

142

the glory and the beauty of our simple love
we walk together through the world
while spilling all our love
sharing all our truth
falling across the tables like waters,

i see you walking by,
and i feel
alienated from everyone,
i see you judging who i am
but you haven't met me
i feel time clawing down
on the short remaining days of our lives
i feel so many words
that need to be spoken
and need to be said
before i can tell you
why we are suffering,

and we have the greatest anger
growing inside our hearts
that we've ever felt
we have the greatest
hatred for all of
the darkness
blinding us

143

Harmonie,
walking through the dirty streets,
and breathing in
the smog,

the noise of the bustling people,
the phases of the moon
the shadows over our world,
that follow us
whichever direction we walk,

i dream of the call to come together
which we hear
in the corner of the classrooms
the lecture
we will never stand united
we will never strive for freedom
South Africa is not our land,

the cycle of
every ordeal
in which the immediate world
is more messed up
with each day that goes by

how we are far from education
and learning the language of the other

we walk together through a world
that has forgotten our truth
that has dug its claws into
the heart of the city,

i have never known any other
home but KZN,
i have never truly wanted another home
i was born here
and i will die here

the loneliness of the road
we traverse down and are lost on,
when we forget that
we don't know where we are going

when we dive into the night
before our fearsome journey is ended
before we lie at the stern of the ship
fallen cold and dead,

come and read
these words
before the world becomes consumed in
its own misfortune

144

when we all fall apart,
the pieces scatter to the ends of the earth

when you have forgotten about
the taste of humanity that was remaining in me
you fall down into the avenues
of wasted years

the marching crowds
through the cities
where we
look out from the top of a building we climbed
and shout words
of violence

and shout words
of echoing degeneracy

and the voices shout back at us,
in an even uglier tone

and then we fall far from the top of the building from
the rocks they have thrown at us,
and then we hit the ground hard
and are carried away
to a place where it is better to be lost
than to be found

you
are
the
never ending
dream, i have
in which i fall
and become so close
to feeling hopeful

you
are
the
always present
shadow
across the hospital floor
where our worlds fall apart
but no other worlds are slain

as long as i can
show you the portrait
of the world

and you see those in the streets
starving
and those who are
as real as i am,
who have a peace within
their souls
and are ready
to sleep forever

i miss the dreams
of silent and beautiful things

i miss the memories
mementos, reminders
that we are still
alive in the same room,

in my apartment,
so much noise
from the party up the stairs
and
i have been swallowed by loneliness
and bliss of times long gone

i dream all night
about her sky blue eyes,
i toss and turn,
i sink and yearn
for the emancipation
i will never feel
when we are lectured

by the ones who are
persecuting us,
when we are living
in a world
where everyone is blinded
from the explosion
of the H-Bomb
and they were simply sitting
in traffic
waiting to get home and to
face the next day
but nothing could have shielded their eyes
from what was caving in on them,

the chaos that is in the world
as we pack our bags
and we leave
and we never return to our old home,
and then the skies turn gray
and then black
and the tornado destroys
our old home
and we crave a different world
than the one we've always known
we crave a more temperate love
than the one we've always
inhaled
we have learned to shy away
from those
who take extreme sides
or who are so fixed in their opinions
that they cannot see
the life through the eyes
of the ones on the other side of the room,

148

we continue to live
we continue to thrive
we have risen out of the slums,
and into your dreams,
we have risen out of the mundane
and into the bright
and glorious world

we have just arrived in the new city
and set up our tent
and we are not at all ready to leave
we are walking through the streets of the city,
we are
dusting off the salt from our boots
when you do not accept us
or even understand us

149

addicted to the sound of
the birds,
and the breath of the stars
the light that comes from the stars inebriates
this room,
frees all the world
the birds land on the stars
and they guide us to the stars
and we fall in love,
with the sensations
that intoxicate us

150

i will be so empowered
by the words she spoke
that she will
be my voice,
she will be my message
that is only just now being shared with the rest of the world

151

we sing anthems in the pitch black night
we have forgotten the words
that were so close to our hearts in our youth
they spoke to us
words of human equality,
love has been lost in the
deep black night
and we never chased after that love
truth had been spoken
truth was never recovered
when i lost Harmonie
in that night as well,
when we floated through the avenues
of a life lived with nothing left to lose,
we walked out the front door of our lives
and dreamed about
acquiring riches
and not living on the street
but we became the kings
and the queens of the slums,
we became the rulers of the world
of the disenfranchised

we wander through the forests
we walked together in
places that came alive
but only in our minds

the falling leaves,
autumn has come
and i do not know where the summer has gone,
i do not know good health
and good life because they are such a distant fantasy,

i walk the streets of the suburbs,
the town run down,
trash, littering all up and down these streets
where i wish i could feel you close against my heart,
where i dive without question
into doubt
and the spirit of the fall
is a memory,
a feeling that cannot ever leave me,
because you were once so close to me
and we held each other so close,
the nations are divided,
we walk all different roads,
and none of them arrive at the same destination
but none of the paths lead out of hell,

listen to me from outside the shell
of your car,
where you sit at the gas station

i have just enough money to fill up my tank
and i drive away,

ditch my car,
and walk alone as the cold does not subside
as the trees are not shielding the darkness from my face

we dream of the different lives we could have lived

155

as i continue walking down the dead-end street
i let the night encompass me in its shroud

as i remember the things that were so warm,
i shiver in this cold
and bring my hands back to the burning trash container
and warm up my fingers
and i speak to no one but the frigid air,
and i listen to no one but the spirit of the passing time,
i hear no one walking in the abode of loneliness

CD #4

we were on the flight together,
your hand
on my thigh,
our hearts in the clouds,
our lives on the line,
our souls were enclosed,
our war we wage
together,

and we know the world
has grown so small,
and the world is the world

our emotions told us
that as we became lost
we swallowed our doubts
we no longer
were in love
with old dreams
we were estranged from the towns we were
most familiar with

the people we used to know would look at us
and not recognize us, at all

i feel your touch,
i feel the rhythm the movement of the songs,
the lull voices
the warm embrace,
the place where we find and hold all inspiration,
the place where we dig so deep into our dirt
that we know we will never be clean again,
we do not move because of logic
we move because of what we feel
we burn with unfathomable passions,
we write down what we feel
and then remember what we were feeling

the shockwave that
falls over us,
when we realize
with utter abandon
how fragile
the beauty is,

how you could
speak its name
and it would break
and the pieces would be shattered all across
the world
and you would never be able to find
any of these pieces ever again

because the pieces form an image
unlike any painting i've seen
or wanted to paint myself

what if the only life you've known was a nightmare?
what would you do if
time was uncontrollably moving,
toward a nightmare that you would never be prepared for?
if the warm embraces you feel would never be felt again

where there is art,
there is truth,
there is something that alters the world
in the most fundamental way
there is destiny fulfilled
and life completed and found its source,

158

i wrote a poem about
the time we first met,
    the reconciliation
        of the last
           broken
      piece
   of heaven,
        before
    it falls into its abyss

i wrote a poem about how my lips press against yours

and you feel absolutely conformed to beauty
as we transition from one moment of joy
to another moment of exaltation,
to the soaring heights of the stars

   you feel the words flow like water
      across the pages of a life we dreamed of
living together
you feel the words written summon more joy
than you ever thought could exist

   you feel the vampire nation,
      become human once again,
        and sing in the joy
          of its own salvation
        and all of your enemies bow
   before your feet

we will understand truths
scholars will never understand
we will understand truths the politicians will never experience
our activism
spills our lives across the floor of the National Assembly

15.9

irrational,
pure
and true
love

> i feel
> love drawing me,
> toward the light
>
> i feel
> love calling me
> in this dark night

beside me,
with me
inside me,
holding me so close
the wind that clutters in through our bedroom door
like the voices of the mourning breeze
lamenting each passing day
that draws us further away from the other

you look into the night and breathe
from the abandoned parking lot,
to the unfinished bridges in KZN,
to the life we call for
to the feeling of fulfillment
and lacking nothing

there is joy flooding all of these things
there is life inhabiting all of these things

the dead nation comes alive
and walks the streets wondering what had happened
while it had fallen asleep,
it wondered why the world had changed so much
and then realized that someone had possessed its own body

and done horrible things
and then the Nation spent its entire life seeking reconciliation
and never found it

160

all sense of rationality is gone,
in a world
where we don't reach across the aisle,
we don't reach anywhere at all,

we forget the name of the one we loved more than anything

and we have forgotten all about the experience

all of our dreams
lead
to unanswered questions
because these questions could never be answered
even if we tried to answer them between now
and the end of all time

the things we longed to experience together
will only be experienced apart,
the dreams we longed to be closer than they would ever be
have slipped so far away from our hands
that they have no knowledge of hands,
or what they can do
or what they are even for,
because hands were meant to hold,
love was meant to thrive

161

when the entire world forgets
that you exist,
                              follow me
into the future

162

my criminal lover, Liefie
the only exciting lover
that came into my life
how i can break off with
the one i was never in love with
and fall after you
feeling fulfilled,
always loved

and i'm looking forward to spending
the rest of my life with you

163

i walked through the graveyard
and contemplated the lives that had gone before

164

we are afraid of being rejected,

by the ones that are closest to us

we have forfeited a long and comfortable life,
we have grown so emotional toward
the things that are only temporary
and which we cannot hold
for even a single instant before it vanishes

i started painting the portraits on the screen,
commission work,
a new way of art
that portrays
the details of what i am feeling
in a single image,

166

we hear the music that emboldens us
to march through the streets
with our empty hearts
that can be filled with anything

167

Harmonie's beautiful
blue and fathomless
stirring eyes,
are what i gazed into
with my hands on her face
with the comfort of home
and joy i found with her,
with the worlds that are
envisioned when i look at her,
with the passing years
we will give new meaning
to every day of the year
because we will spend these days together

the hue of the
sky,
like the same depth in her eyes,
the warmth of the oceans
like the peace
found in her embrace,
the brazen lies

we hear every evening
constitute
a declaration
of ignorance

while we stand by the power lines
during the load shedding
shaking in disbelief that both of us are still alive,
and that the chaos of the
converging worlds
brought us here
to a moment where we can lie down together
and look at the trees
and then the power lines
and see the stars and distant worlds shining above

we lose our minds when we fall in love,
we lose our lives eventually so i will lose everything i have
and pass it on to you

i came home to her
where within the world of so much turmoil,
there is peace in a quiet room,
there is joy when we can lie down alone
and dream together,
and let the TV light guide us to sleep,
and let the unhinged anthems of nations
guide us into a world where
the nations do not exist in their current form,
we are guided by little miracles
into lands where we are no longer stranded,
into a comfortable life where
we will not be standing in the middle of Durban with no
phone
and no wallet and no plane ticket home,

168

so many years ago
we were crawling out of our own fears
and becoming the persons
we always wanted to be
with no regrets,
with no pain
and no despair

169

i struggle to put to words
what is so close inside my soul
what could never be understood by any human person
living or dead

170

every time the sun rises
it draws us closer
to our promised and uncertain future,

every time i call your name
it brings us closer to our future
together,
when you will hold me and never let go,
when words take a tangible form
that can be felt like skin against skin,
when all i want to do
is express what i feel
and never stop expressing these same truths
when music is the motion
that forever underlines our lives
and makes us move forward in motion
when we look inside ourselves
and see immovable truth
and such depth that we could stare
at it forever and never stop

learning more about it,

171

when no one has embraced the melodies
that we understand,
we will become closer to each other
   in the fact that we are
the only two people in the world
that no one understands,

172

with our hearts open wide,
we offer all we have to a world
that had forsaken us,

with our minds willing to learn anything
that exudes truth,
is real and graspable,
we fall after you

173

we crave miracles
in a world that no longer believes
and people lost their minds
when one actually happened

174

we lie in separate rooms,
the darkness seeps through into
these rooms
where we wait for the end of all time

175

the cruelty of the passing time
when we are still
and always will be uncertain
of our chances
of obtaining a normal life together,

176

counting down the days
until we are understood by anyone
or even listened to

177

i feel
desperate
to express
the truth inside my soul

178

i am reaching out and feeling your skin
i am reaching out and touching
your soul,
and i say all the words
i was too afraid to share with anyone else,

179

i warm my hands in front of the fire,
i let the warmth take me over
and i dream
that life was not like this
        that just as the world
        was about to turn against you,
        it stopped and wondered what it was
        doing, or why it wanted to

and never persecuted you again
and i dreamt that people listened
to the words of the poets
and those of the artists
and that these words transformed
the nation into one with no violence
no poverty
and no despair
and that we weren't slowly losing our homes
without compensation,
losing the things we held so close
to us, with no regard for what they were
or how valuable they were to us

180

you will write our story
and tell the world
every detail
of the emotions
it thought were meaningless,

181

as the night became longer
we started counting the seconds
as the fear became unbearable
we started feeling so numb
and unable to feel anything again

182

life without the turmoil
of every day

when we are stranded in the middle of
nowhere
we will still walk whatever direction,
hoping to find each other

eventually, if we walk far enough,

183

after we wait,
we give up

after sighing
comes exasperation

after music comes silence

after gunshots in the city
there are vain sirens
during lonely nights
we are blind,

the whole world is enclosed in a single soul,
the whole world burns when a soul burns,
the places your lips have kissed
my skin still burn
your hands trail across my body
fingers leaving scorch marks everywhere they touch
my body aches for more

184

Harmonie's eyes like
portals,
into a lonely world
her hair like
a shroud
that covers
the darkness
and traps it
so that it
never leaves
and never tempts us

again,
her warmth like
celebration
of coming home
to a home
that would never
forsake us
her lips sweet as honey
raging against the unstoppable embrace of death

185

"with a kiss
i die"
and fall down,
into
the echoing halls of the forgotten
and am never remembered,
except in the libraries
of those who have
believed in love
some may come to those shelves
and find our book.
and when they read it from cover
to cover,
they will know how
to save the world from certain disaster,
if only they have the courage
to open it...

186

i'm here
you're there
my heart aches
yours breaks
we're spinning in this circle
each day over and over
it's the same thing

it doesn't change
we want change

i want you
to feel
so completely free
from this cycle
that when you take
my hand, you will
certainly be able
to grasp it
and follow me
step by step
into a life
where we experience
not only truth
but also the deepest
fulfillment,
and when we fall deeper
into the thriving
sea of the love we found
together, we never reach the
bottom

187

with each night that passes,
i lie down
and let it vanish
and when it is gone
i greet the new day
with all of the bruises
scrapes and cuts that come
with the new months
and i don't complain
i just live
and shut the part of my brain
off that cares

if it is cut
or if it is left open for the rest
of the world to see,
because i am naked
with my words
more than i could ever
be naked with my body,
i have more freedom when
i am writing
than i will have anywhere else in the world
typing these words
that will be read all over the world
as we wait for the world
to get bored of its routine,
we are exhausted
and then we dream and let more years
pass, until
the world ignores us
and never hears anything we are saying
until we demonstrate
that no one in the world
has greater love than us

188

the days when the world goes quiet
because there is no more dissonance
because the world gave up
on trying to write a beautiful symphony
and all it could produce
were clanging noises and discordance
when your tied tongue is loosened
it breaks through the silence
and sings beautiful words
that the world had never heard before
but had dreamed of hearing
and then the world learns your song
and plays it as a symphony everywhere

189

when we forget
so many words
and forget everything
that we ever learned in school
and unlearn language
and learn a new language
and forget the people we
lived with before
and live in an entirely new city
where we write love letters
about the beauty of the world
and finding yourself
and becoming someone
you always wanted to become
your entire life
but were not brave enough to admit these truths
to yourself

190

into the dark
we fall
and i fall after you,

we are bitterly weeping
for the loss of the nation of light
when we have descended so far
into the empire of the shadows
that we will never go up
to where we can barely see the light breaking
through the surface of the chilling water

191

love covers us like
        dew in the morning

we lose our hope
in a world
where hope is derided
because we are not
brave enough
to stand out from the crowd
and to
fight for a future
we are not sure we will
ever find,
where hatred is louder
than love,
where death is easier
than life,

my stars touch your birds
and your birds carry my stars
on their wings
on their journey
to a universe
where they never have to worry
about shining over a broken world

i want you
in
desperate
moments
to be here
and not only to understand
but to experience
the world
through my eyes
and the eyes of all

195

you feel the days pass
again
and
the world passes away like
time is lapsing

196

the mountains
where we are alive
and feel the same things
as countless souls
that traversed here before us

197

i held you so close
and didn't let go
and
held on to this moment
for the rest of my days

198

when we inhale
we take in every breath slowly

199

when fear is struck in our hearts
and we fall away
from the image of God,
we rejoice in the face
of the crowds
who call for division
and death,
we are caught up

in the moments when we know
we could become anything
and write our story
in the depth of the winter
when everything
is frozen over
and we cannot move our fingers
quickly enough to write,
when we are buried in our own tears,
because we drowned in them
when the nation falls in
on itself from
inhaling a little bit too much despair
when we learn to resist the panic
when every year that passes
is a marathon
of doubts one after another,
and the hope we had is lost on
its way home to us
and never finds us,
when we are broken
and cannot find the instructions
to put ourselves back together
when Harmonie sings to me
and i hear her overwhelming
beautiful and lamenting voice,
she is more American than me,
she is more addicted to
the light of freedom of speech
she is more enthralled with
living a simple life
when our families abandon us,
there will be nowhere else to turn,
when all of our things are on the street
and we cannot carry them,
when we fear for our very lives
and we are threatened
by the burning rage of a world
that never understood us

when we wait in the moonlight
for the stars to disappear
so that the world is completely dark and we can sleep
and leave this world
and travel to a world
we will only experience in our dreams
where we are still loved
and understood,
when all we need is one more person
to listen
before the whole world
hears
and turns the other direction
from which it was walking
and we no longer want to live forever
at least not in this world
we do not understand what is broken
within our world,
we do not know how to describe it to others
so we lock the doors to the rooms of
our own hearts
and fight against the chains
they shackle us with
but we are never able to leave the room,
we are never able to walk so far away
that we will never be found again by our enemies,
i have so many thoughts i cannot explain,
i have so much truth i cannot convince you of,
i have seen so much cruelty, which i don't
believe is real

fading like the light of the stars
dying like the fate
of those lost in the darkness of warmth
when the bombs blow off the shell,
creating craters in the earth,
within our hearts there used
to be joy
when we would
never be able to express
what we were feeling
because it was too painful to speak
callouses on our hands
bruises on our torsos,
stripes across our backs,
cruelty, animosity
and we run away from the masters of slaves

having so much passion that the world
would never talk about it,
having so much love
the world would never experience it,
having so much truth the world would destroy you,
craving revolution so much
the world started a crusade against you,

being so loud and upfront
with all of this,
that the world tried to suppress you and when the world tried
to push you down
you only pushed back with your words,
you
knew how short your life would be,
together we would be
laughing about the world
and how we knew it would treat us,
racism is beyond absurdity,
depth we fell so far into

that we would never have hope of returning
to the state we were in before

with just a single touch we
felt it
we understood each other,
we were at odds with the world,
whether you are
near or far,
i believe my love covers these oceans
feelings of warmth and security would
flood our hearts,
a world without anxiety,
a future filled with glory
where the trees reach out for love,
like when i reach out for your hand
and you take it

when you show me the beauty in the world
i follow and fall more deeply in love
with you,
when i kiss you, all i can think
about is the difference between heaven
and mortality
and how i wish it will never end
when we go to new and exciting places,
i realize that anywhere with you is my
favorite place in the world
when i am far from you i want to be closer
and when we're in the same room,
i want to be closer
and when our skin is touching i want to
be closer
and i cherish your breath
more than wine
and more than gold
more than life
and more than the scarce warmth
in the coldness of winter

i cannot imagine my life without you,
you are kind,
you are loving
and pure
and i would never need to tell you
these things

201

when your heart was broken,
i stitched it back together
with my own hands
and they were covered in your blood
and then i felt you breathing
across my neck
and then i heard you sleeping
and then i found you in your dreams
and spoke to you
and loved you in those dreams
until you would never forget
the life we lived in our dreams
and then when you woke up
you would write about this experience
forever until the world would greet
you again with all its unwelcoming
glances, but you knew it wasn't your world
that was rejecting you,
we could live as if the world was foreign to us,
as if it was never familiar or friendly
as if we were starving to find
a world where we could thrive in
the streets of the cities
in which we would hear the whimpering voices of people
suffering long
in the shadows
of people dreaming of a world like
the one we had dreamed about
and we led them out of the dull world

with us and we built a nation
and this nation led to a kingdom
and this kingdom
to a world without end

202

the birds outside are conversing
they are telling each other
stories
we never understood,
about the free and open sky
and those stars of yours
that they land on and find peace
with, but which i would never
understand

with you and me everything
is perfect

204

you hear my truth when i whisper it
deep into your ears
and your whole self is exonerated

205

we have held each other so close
and we will never even
when time expires
willingly forget about each other

the danger of love
is that it never gives up
never gives in,
never lets go of you
finds you where you are in the shadows
and draws you into the light
love is so incredibly dangerous
that the crusade against it
never ends until
the forces of the dark lord are overthrown
until the light of morning
pierces in through the castle
until my truth spills into the hearts
of all those who
not long ago were at war with us,
until you know the dreams we have
are the anthem of our lives,
that must be understood
and inhaled into the minds of the ones
who were forgetting
about their loved ones

207

South Africa
my first home,
where i will never belong
but where i will always rage against the
time that wastes away our lives
until we have no way to hold on to anything

the dream of the poet
the ecstasy of the poet
who became a dreamer

the despair that each moment brings
inside the prison
where we are afraid of being
carried away one last time

the fear of the edge of the knife,
the fear of what is inside the soul
that drives them to use the knife,
when we are standing
as souls separated and desperate to
understand
and if only we could find each other
we would escape from the prison together,
we would destroy the hunger
of these fires that devour everything
in the forest we used to call home,

we would fall so deeply in love
that we would never want to not be
in love ever again,

you would feel peace deep inside your bones,
where for a moment you wait
for the fear to pass,
for the riots in the streets to clear
for the riot police to leave
and you walk the streets
that are now empty with the glass
and broken Molotov cocktails
all over the ground
broken, everywhere
and you walk these streets
until you come to your old home
and you find it burning
and then you watch the news and see
everyone talking about your death
and that you were pregnant
when you died
but violence knows no bounds

and that when you died South Africa
did not mourn
or weep but turned the other way
and never repented
and continued on its course
and then i walked across the oceans
and saw my Liefie in a boxcar,
traveling to another city,
weeping
and losing my picture as the wind blew
it away
and it was never seen by anyone again,
and then my Liefie walked for miles
until he was greeted by the cold winter
where he rested and never rose up,

i was sitting under the tree
in my youth
and i was writing
in a journal
all of my thoughts,

in my youth i was listening
closely to the spirit between
the light and the expanse of the sky,
i was staring at the sky
and i was
waiting for someone to speak
words that would describe what i was feeling

i was waiting for the world to find grace
while it was freefalling away from it,
i was wanting to sing joyfully
and triumphantly
about the things i had experienced
in such a way that every living person
in the world would understand them

Joseph Leo Hickey lives in Virginia. He is the author of seven other poetry books, including *Baptism of Apathy*, *Unity*, *Love Poems at The End of Our Lives*, *Liefie*, *The Last Poem*, *Purity: Redeemed* and *The Penultimate Poems*. He is currently 27 years old.

His upcoming books are *I Know Nothing but Miracles*, *The Revenant*, and *Baptism of Apathy (Volumes 2-14)*.

YouTube: allthestarsaredead

joseph@melodiumhouse.com

www.ingramcontent.com/pod-product-compliance
Lightning Source LLC
LaVergne TN
LVHW051704080426
835511LV00017B/2712